STEROIDS

STEROIDS

Dangerous Game

Lisa Angowski Rogak

Lerner Publications Company • Minneapolis

For Christopher Rogak

All words that appear in **bold** type are defined in a glossary that
begins on page 51.

LIBRARY OF CONGRESS CATALOGING-IN-PUBLICATION DATA

Rogak, Lisa.
   Steroids : dangerous game / Lisa Angowski Rogak.
     p.   cm.
   Includes index.
   Summary: Discusses the use and dangers of steroids and other
drugs used by athletes.
   ISBN 0-8225-0048-5
   1. Anabolic steroids—Juvenile literature. 2. Doping in sports—
Juvenile literature. [1. Steroids. 2. Drug abuse. 3. Athletes—Drug
use.] I. Title.
RC1230.R64 1992
362.29'08'8796—dc20   91-46896
                                                  CIP
                                                   AC

Manufactured in the United States of America

1   2   3   4   5   96   95   94   93   92

Contents

1
What Are Steroids?

The late summer sun warmed the backs of the varsity football players after the first scrimmage of the season. On a bench on the sidelines, Jeff took a swig from his water bottle. He passed it to Brandon without taking his eyes off the players on the field.

Out of the corner of his eye, Brandon watched Jeff. College scouts from the Big Ten schools had been courting Jeff for a whole year already. "I wish I had his strength on the field," Brandon thought.

Donna, one of Jeff's many female admirers, walked by, waving. Jeff waved back.

"And it sure doesn't hurt him off the field, either," Brandon thought. He tilted back his head as he took a long drink of water. He let out a deep sigh.

Jeff turned to Brandon. "Hey, what's the matter?" he

7

asked. "You handled yourself pretty well out there today."

"Oh, nothing," said Brandon. "It's just that I'm starting to think about college next year. My parents don't have a lot of money, and there's not much chance of me getting a football scholarship. I mean, look at me." Brandon pointed to his padded frame. "I'll never be big enough to get any attention from even the state school." He scuffed the dirt with his foot.

Jeff put an arm around his friend. "Listen," he whispered into Brandon's ear. "I have a secret. Me and Coach were going to keep quiet for a while longer, but now that you brought it up—"

Brandon raised his head. "What are you talking about?"

The whistle blew, and Jeff got up and brushed off his pants. "Juice, man. You've got to get on the juice to get anywhere in football."

"Juice? What's juice?" Brandon asked. He started jogging onto the field alongside Jeff.

"You know, juice. 'Roids," Jeff said, then lowered his voice. "Steroids, man. Where've you been? Half the team's on them."

"Steroids?" Brandon asked loudly. A few of his teammates turned to look at him. "You take steroids?" he asked, whispering this time.

"I have to. Coach says that's the only way you're going to get noticed in the game." Jeff smiled. "Besides, look at my cheering squad."

Jeff waved again to Donna, who was sitting in the bleachers. She waved back. Three rows behind her sat two men in suits with clipboards on their laps. They waved at Jeff too. "I was wondering what took you so long," he added to Brandon.

Brandon felt a little dizzy. "Jeff, I don't know. Aren't they supposed to be bad for you? Aren't they drugs?"

Suddenly Jeff got angry. "Man, what are you, stupid? Can't you see everything I have now? My life is set, and I'm not going to listen to you tell me that it's not."

Jeff softened and put his arm around Brandon's shoulder again. "Look, I just want you to have the same chances I've had. I'll help you," he said. "And so will Coach, I know he will. If you start a cycle now, you'll be in shape for the last game of the season, when the scouts will be here again. The schools will come after *you*, too. How about it?" They took their places on the field for exercises.

"I don't know," said Brandon. "I'll have to think about it."

Facts about Steroids

You've probably heard about **steroids,** but, like Brandon, you might not know exactly what they are. You may have heard a news report about an athlete who has abused laboratory-produced, or **synthetic,** steroids. And if you've studied biology, you may know about another kind of steroid—a chemical that is produced naturally in the human body. This book is concerned primarily with abuse of synthetic steroids. But to understand the problem of steroid abuse, you need to know how both kinds of steroids work.

Steroids exist naturally in all animals and plants. In

the human body, steroids control growth, **metabolism** (the process by which the body turns food into energy and living tissue), and blood chemistry. The two main kinds of natural steroids are the corticosteroids and the sex steroids.

Corticosteroids are released by the **adrenal glands**, small organs located near the kidneys. Corticosteroids help to regulate protein and **carbohydrate** metabolism. They also influence the body's mineral and water balance in both males and females.

The **sex steroids** are also produced by the adrenal glands, in small quantities, and are present in the bodies of both men and women. Women's **ovaries** produce additional steroids: **progesterone** and **estrogens**. Progesterone and estrogens are called female sex steroids or female **hormones**. Men's bodies produce **testosterone** in the **testes**. Testosterone is called a male sex steroid or hormone.

A person's sex is defined by the **primary sexual characteristics**—ovaries in women and testes in men. But it is the amount of each sex steroid in a person's body that determines the **secondary sexual characteristics**—breast development, high voice, and smooth skin in females, and large muscles, deep voice, and facial hair in males.

A part of the brain called the **hypothalamus** controls the secretion of steroids. In a healthy body, the hypothalamus causes the ovaries, testes, and adrenal glands to produce and release steroids in proper amounts according to a person's sex.

Because our bodies don't always work right,

scientists have developed artificial steroids for medical use. Synthetic corticosteroids, for instance, can reduce tissue swelling. They are used to treat arthritis and soft tissue injuries such as muscle strain and muscle tears. **Anabolic steroids**, which are similar to the male sex hormone testosterone, are used to promote muscle growth. Both corticosteroids and anabolic steroids are legally manufactured for medical use.

Steroids are also used routinely and legally in veterinary medicine. They are used in meat production, to increase muscle in cattle and thereby produce extra-lean beef, and they are given to show horses, racehorses, and race dogs to increase their muscle mass and muscle strength.

But people have used steroids for purposes other than those for which they were intended. People especially have abused anabolic steroids. Though intended to make sick people strong, the drugs are often used by healthy people, mainly athletes, who simply want to promote muscle growth. These artificial steroids are sometimes known as "juice" and " 'roids." Steroid users are often called "chemical athletes."

How Do Anabolic Steroids Work?

Anabolic steroids are manufactured in pill form and in a liquid form that can be injected into the body. A user will take steroids for a specific period of time called a cycle—usually two months. He or she then either reduces the dose or stops steroid use for a few weeks before beginning the next cycle. Whether taken orally or by injection, anabolic steroids travel into the bloodstream, and then into the body's cells. If the steroids go to muscle cells, the steroids may promote muscle tissue growth.

Muscles grow larger when exercise breaks down proteins in the muscle cells and the body rebuilds the muscle tissue. If a steroid user engages in strenuous, muscle-building exercise, such as weightlifting, the steroids will increase the amount of protein that is sent to the muscle cells for the rebuilding process. Without strenuous exercise, however, steroids are useless in a healthy body.

Steroids can actually help to build muscles. Steroids also allow injuries to heal faster and may reduce the amount of time an athlete needs to rest between workouts. Anabolic steroids may also increase aggression, which can make an athlete want to work out longer and harder than a nonuser. Whether the steroids actually increase a user's strength is not certain, however. Bigger muscles do not necessarily mean stronger muscles. The **placebo effect**—in which an athlete's performance improves merely because she or he believes it will—may be responsible for some of the improvement an athlete shows after beginning to use steroids.

2
Steroid Use and Abuse

Kathy and Lynn leaned toward the bathroom mirror as they fixed their hair between classes. They were discussing the upcoming track meet. Suddenly Robin walked into the bathroom, and the two girls abruptly stopped talking.

Robin had just transferred to Lockwood High a few months before. But she had already become the track team's new star, an overnight sensation.

"Hi guys," Robin said. She walked by them to another mirror. "Looking forward to Saturday?"

"Yeah," both girls said, keeping their eyes down.

Robin opened her purse. "You know," she said quietly while rummaging through the purse for a comb, "I don't understand why everyone is against me. I come to practice and I work out just as hard as everybody else." She looked up at Kathy and Lynn. "I just have a little extra help."

Kathy and Lynn looked at each other, then at Robin.

"Come over here," Robin said, putting a hand in her purse. She pulled out a prescription bottle. "My times were worse than yours before a doctor gave me these."

The two girls stared at Robin. Then Lynn walked over to Robin and took the bottle from her. The label said *Winstrol.* She opened the bottle and spilled a few capsules into her palm.

"What are you doing?" Kathy demanded of Robin. "Are those steroids?" Her voice echoed off the bathroom walls. "For your information, steroids are illegal. I'm going to tell Coach and she'll have you kicked off the team. You might even get suspended from school!"

"They're not illegal if I have a prescription," said Robin. Her voice was calm. "And anyway, if you do tell, I'll just deny it."

Kathy glared at Robin, then at Lynn. "Using steroids just isn't playing fair. Put them back, Lynn," she commanded. "We're leaving."

Lynn looked at Kathy. "No. I want to stay for a minute. After all, Robin's times *are* the best."

Kathy snorted in disgust. "I don't believe you, Lynn. It's *cheating*. If you swallow even one of those pills, I swear I'll never talk to you again." Out in the hall, the bell rang for the next class to start. Kathy stomped out of the room.

The two girls listened as Kathy's footsteps rang down the hall. Lynn turned back to Robin, the pills still in her palm, and said, "Tell me more."

The History of Steroid Use

Anabolic steroids were first developed for medical purposes during the 1930s. During World War II (1939–1945), the German army reportedly gave anabolic steroids to soldiers to make them more aggressive in combat. After the war, doctors in Europe and the United States frequently used steroids to treat anemia—a blood disorder—and malnutrition, and to help patients recover more quickly from surgery.

By the late 1940s, bodybuilders in Eastern Europe were taking testosterone in various forms. In the 1950s, athletes used anabolic steroids to improve their performance in international competition. With the government's approval, coaches in the Soviet Union gave anabolic steroids to their athletes, particularly weightlifters and shot-putters. When other athletes and coaches took notice of the Soviets' winning records (Soviet weightlifters won seven medals at the 1952 Olympics), athletes in many countries began to experiment with steroid use.

In 1956, American doctor John B. Ziegler worked with a drug company to produce anabolic steroids in the United States. Professional athletes, particularly football players, began using steroids as early as the 1960s. The health dangers of steroids were not yet recognized, and athletes obtained steroids legally from their team doctors. When state laws against steroid use were passed in the 1960s, a black market, or illegal trade, for steroids developed. Steroids eventually found their way into school athletics, at both the college and high school levels. And during the 1980s, steroid use spread outside the athletic world. Recently steroids have been used more and more by nonathletes, including teens.

Who Uses Steroids?

Athletes in almost every kind of sport have been known to take steroids. Men and women and girls and boys take steroids, although it's more common for males to use the drugs than females. Athletes may use various types and amounts of anabolic steroids, depending upon their sport. In football, weightlifting, or bodybuilding—sports in which brute strength and large muscles are desirable—athletes sometimes take heavy doses of anabolic steroids. Wrestlers and swimmers might take smaller amounts, and track-and-field athletes may take even less. While shot put, discus, and javelin throwers may use steroids heavily, a long-distance runner does not need muscle mass for endurance.

Drug testing officials at the Olympic Games estimate that up to 80 percent of male athletes in track-and-field have used steroids at one time or another to compete on the international level. Football is another sport in which steroid abuse has been rampant. One former player with the National Football League said that in NFL training camps in the early 1960s, coaches and trainers placed bowls heaped full of steroid tablets on dining tables, and players sprinkled the tablets on their cereal like sugar. In September 1990, the NFL suspended 17 athletes for either taking anabolic steroids or distributing them to their teammates.

During the inquiry that led up to the suspensions, one player estimated that 75 percent of NFL athletes used steroids regularly.

Surveys show that in the late 1980s, 6 percent of high school athletes and up to 20 percent of college athletes admitted taking steroids. Another recent survey of high school students shows that nonathletes are taking steroids as well. Nearly one-third of those who said they used steroids were not involved in any sport.

Why Do People Use Steroids?

Sports have become a big industry in the last 25 years. The pressure on an athlete to win is tremendous. A gold medal in the Olympics can mean millions of dollars to athletes, coaches, managers, sponsors, and even countries. A championship team can bring an up-to-date training facility and a top coaching staff to an otherwise middle-ranked college. A top high school quarterback can have his choice of schools and scholarships, with a possible shot at the pros later on. A coach with a winning record can often have his or her pick of jobs at top schools.

When the competition gets tough, some athletes will do almost anything to come out on top. Shaving just a few seconds off a race time can make the difference between first and fifth place for a sprinter or a swimmer. If a drug promises to give results, many coaches and athletes will not hesitate to use it.

Some coaches and doctors estimate that anabolic steroids boost a professional athlete's performance by

1–2 percent. Some coaches also believe that if an entire team is using anabolic steroids, the athletes will be able to perform as much as 10 percent better than if they didn't use the drugs. Such statements, of course, do not take into account the placebo effect. Athletes who take anabolic steroids may have increased confidence that they will perform better, and therefore they train with extra energy. The extra-hard training, not the drugs, may be what actually creates winning athletes.

An increasing number of people take anabolic steroids not because they are involved in sports, but because they want to look strong and muscular. The media continually bombard us with the message that to be sexy, one must have a fit, muscular body. Rambos and Terminators are portrayed as male ideals. Many young men take this message to heart and do whatever is necessary to achieve a similar look.

In the past, training with weights was the only way to build muscles. But some people find that anabolic steroids can help them achieve their ideal much faster. What they may not know is that without strenuous exercise, steroids won't add muscle—just extra weight and a bloated, puffy look. People also may not realize that steroids do more harm to the body than good.

We live in a culture that accepts casual drug use. It's considered perfectly acceptable to swallow aspirin and many other types of drugstore painkillers. Alcohol is a legal and widely used mood-altering drug. Many people do not associate steroids with other illegal drugs, such as heroin and cocaine. Because it's easy to buy steroids on the black market, the threat of arrest and punishment may seem slight. Many people have not received adequate warnings about the health risks that steroids pose. And some athletes decide that winning—and the rewards that go with it—are more important than their future health. But playing with steroids is a dangerous game.

3
The Dangers of Anabolic Steroids

The halls in school were buzzing. Swimmer Jack Turner, a former Olympic gold-medalist, was scheduled to talk at a special afternoon assembly.

Mike was especially excited. Mike was on the varsity swim team, and this morning during practice, he was sure he swam faster than ever before. Each time Mike touched the side of the pool, he imagined he was Jack Turner winning the gold medal.

The swim coach had watched Mike practice. As Mike climbed out of the pool, his coach was waiting with some news. "Mike," he said, holding back a smile, "I think I can convince Jack Turner to stay and watch you at this afternoon's practice."

That seemed like ages ago now, but finally it was 2:00. As Mike followed his classmates into the auditorium, he shut out the noise around him. He took his seat and watched the podium where his hero soon would speak.

The lights went down and the room grew quiet. "There he is!" Mike thought, as a man dressed in a suit walked onto the stage.

"Good afternoon, everyone," the man boomed into the microphone. "I'm Jack Turner. I know you probably want to hear about how exciting it was to win a gold medal at the Olympics. You might also like to hear about the famous people I've met since then. But I'm here to talk with you about something much more important."

As Jack Turner paused, Mike noticed that he swallowed hard. Mike shivered as he wondered what could be so important.

Jack continued. "I'm here to talk to you about the dangers of steroids and other drugs in sports. I fooled myself for years, thinking steroids were the secret to my success as a swimmer. I thought I couldn't win, compete, or even live without them. But now I've found out that I can't live *with* them. Last month I was diagnosed with liver cancer."

A jolt went through Mike's body. He couldn't believe what Jack was saying. He used steroids? And now he was going to die because of it?

Mike didn't listen to the rest of Jack's speech. He thought instead about his own swimming career. Jack Turner's career seemed so phony now.

"I don't want him to watch me at practice this afternoon," Mike thought.

Physical Dangers and Side Effects

Anabolic steroids are powerful drugs. Like any medication, they can produce a number of negative side effects, or undesired reactions. Some side effects last only as long as the drug is being taken. Other side effects are permanent, lasting long after the drug use is stopped.

The temporary side effects of steroid use include high blood pressure, acne, nosebleeds, hair loss, and fluid retention, which can result in bloating, making the body and face appear puffy. Other side effects include a higher tolerance for pain, increased or lowered sexual drive, **sterility, impotence,** increased appetite, and **insomnia.** In male users, anabolic steroids may cause the penis to enlarge and the testicles to shrink.

The permanent, irreversible physical effects of steroid use are much more serious. Because anabolic steroids can increase the levels of fat in the blood, users are at risk for heart attacks and other heart problems. Steroids can cause liver and kidney disease—including cancer and **hepatitis.** A condition called **gynecomastia**—breast development in boys and men—is prevalent among male steroid users. Gynecomastia is permanent, and many men with the condition have had the excess breast tissue surgically removed.

Steroid use can also cause injuries to **tendons,** the cords that attach muscles to bones. While steroids may strengthen muscles, they do nothing to strengthen tendons. As a result, tendons cannot carry the extra weight that users put on, and the tendons can become strained, or they may even rupture.

Injectable steroids and steroids purchased on the black market present additional dangers. Users who share **hypodermic needles** risk getting diseases such as hepatitis B and AIDS. Black market steroids are likely to have been manufactured without any medical supervision and cannot be guaranteed sterile and pure. Often black market dealers sell steroids that were manufactured for veterinary use. Veterinary steroids are often not as pure as those intended for human use, and they are packaged in doses that are inappropriate for the human body. Steroids bought and sold on the black market can also be counterfeit, or phony, and the actual ingredients may be more dangerous than the steroids themselves.

Psychological Effects

Bigger muscles can help increase a person's self-esteem. But the steroids that build those muscles can lead to lowered self-esteem, depression, inability to think clearly, and lack of energy. Medical researchers are also looking at the connection between testosterone levels and aggressive behavior. More and more evidence indicates that high levels of testosterone increase hostility and the potential for violence. While high testosterone levels may not actually cause a person to be violent, they may push someone with aggressive or violent tendencies to act on them.

After one amateur weightlifter on steroids smashed his car into a telephone pole, he admitted that the action was deliberate—he had wanted to see what it would feel like. He even had asked a friend to videotape the crash. A Maryland man who was charged with several burglaries and robberies said his steroid use was to blame. Fits of violence among users have become so common that they have been given a name—" 'roid rages."

The cyclical nature of steroid use—two months on the drugs, one month off—seems to aggravate mood swings. When off the drugs, an athlete may feel so depressed that he or she gets back on the drugs too early. He or she might also take larger doses in order to offset the low moods.

Taking several kinds of steroids at the same time is called **stacking**. Stacking is a common practice that multiplies the risks of steroid use. Steroid use can also lead to use of other drugs—especially those that treat the side effects of steroids. Taking multiple drugs is called **polypharmacy**, and it is a very dangerous practice. Adding to steroid users' health risks is the fact that many people take the drugs without any medical supervision, and they often take the steroids in megadoses—sometimes up to 20 times the recommended dosage.

Teenagers and Steroids

One of the earliest medical uses for anabolic steroids was to promote growth in underdeveloped children. This practice is no longer widespread, since many doctors consider it dangerous. Although steroids encourage muscle growth, they can stop bone growth.

The ends of the leg and arm bones contain a thin disk of **cartilage,** a rubbery tissue, that turns to bone when an adolescent reaches his or her adult height. Steroid use can cause the cartilage to turn prematurely into bone, permanently stunting a teen's growth.

Most boys don't grow to their full height until their late teens. If a boy takes steroids while he is still growing, he may not grow as tall as he normally would have. Just one cycle of steroid use can stunt a teen's growth.

Women and Steroids

A man's body produces about 100 times the amount of testosterone that a woman's body produces. Because women's bodies are not accustomed to high testosterone levels, women who take steroids generally see their bodies change dramatically and rapidly. Even a small dose of steroids can significantly change a woman's body.

Testosterone affects a woman's body in the same way that it does a man's body—that is, it builds muscles *and* produces male characteristics. A female steroid user may find that her facial bone structure actually changes, altering her features. She may grow facial hair, her voice might deepen, her breasts can shrink, and her menstrual cycle might stop. Steroids may also make a woman sterile. More scientific research is needed to understand all the ways steroids affect the body. Research especially needs to be done on the effects of steroids in women. But studies so far indicate that these physical changes are irreversible.

Are Steroids Addictive?

Whether or not anabolic steroids are physically addictive is still in question. Some users have reported feelings of peacefulness while on the drugs and symptoms of withdrawal when they stopped. What researchers are certain about is that steroids are psychologically addictive. Watching one's body change rapidly—whether due to actual steroid use or the placebo effect—can hook a steroid user fast.

Many people who use steroids say that they intend to use the drugs for just a short time, then stop. But they often end up taking drugs for many years. A steroid user who likes the results of the drug—such as increased muscle bulk and improved performance—often cannot stop using it. Bulked-up muscles shrink when drug use is stopped. And an athlete may fear that his or her performance level will drop dramatically without the drugs. An athlete on steroids may lose all confidence in his or her natural athletic ability.

Steroids Are against the Law

The health risks that go along with steroid use prevent some people from using the drugs. It is also illegal in the United States to use steroids without a prescription. Penalties for use vary from fines to imprisonment. There are even penalties for doctors who prescribe anabolic steroids to athletes solely to improve athletic performance. A U.S. doctor who is caught prescribing unnecessary steroids to athletes can have his or her medical license revoked by the American Medical Association.

Steroid users get around the law by purchasing drugs on the black market. Just as there are drug dealers who specialize in selling cocaine and marijuana, some dealers sell illegal drugs to athletes. In many bodybuilding gyms, dealers regularly visit the locker rooms—usually with the full knowledge of the gym owner. Some dealers also sell anabolic steroids through the mail. They have contacts with athletic coaches and the owners and managers of weight-training gyms, who frequently earn a commission, or payment, on every sale.

Other users obtain steroids from a coach or by finding a doctor who will write a prescription. Some users travel to Mexico, where many brands of steroids are sold without a prescription. United States customs agents regularly search for steroids, however, and catch many of those who try to smuggle drugs across the Mexican–U.S. border.

The FBI and U.S. Customs Department have begun to prosecute drug dealers who sell and distribute anabolic steroids. In 1987 California classified steroids as controlled substances, which means that their possession and use must be regulated by law. Many dealers in California have been convicted and sent to prison in the last few years for selling steroids in gyms and through the mail. David Jenkins, a former track star from Great Britain, was convicted of buying counterfeit anabolic steroids in Mexico and distributing them in the United States. In 1987 a ton (2,000 pounds) of steroids valued at $1.5 million was seized at the Canadian border.

The use of steroids to improve athletic performance is also against the rules and codes of ethics of most international sports organizations, including the International Amateur Athletic Federation (IAAF) and the International Olympic Committee (IOC), the governing body of the Olympic Games.

While most sports organizations forbid drug use in competition, governments in many countries have not outlawed the use of anabolic steroids. Instead, some countries—such as Australia and Canada—have issued statements against anabolic steroids and other performance-enhancing drugs. Belgium and Greece are two countries that have passed laws against drug use in sports. Other countries require Olympic athletes to submit to random drug testing year-round.

In the United States, steroids are banned by the National Collegiate Athletic Association (NCAA) and the U.S. Olympic Committee. In professional sports, steroids are specifically prohibited by the National Football League.

4
Drug Testing in Sports

The locker room was unusually quiet. On another day the track-and-field team would be laughing, telling jokes, and talking about the upcoming meet. Instead, the sound of lockers being pulled open and then slammed shut echoed throughout the room.

"What's the matter? Don't they trust us?" Robert was the first to speak. "I can't believe they're going to test us!"

"It's an invasion of privacy," added Danny, the team's star sprinter, from across the room. "I won't be able to have one beer all season!"

"I can't pee into a jar," said Robert. "It's too embarrassing."

"Do you think they'll make us pee in front of somebody?" Chris asked.

29

Nobody answered. The boys continued dressing in silence for a minute.

"Hey, Dave, you've been quiet," said Chris. "What do you think?"

Dave didn't respond. He sat in front of his open locker, staring at his cleats hanging over the door.

"Hey Dave, didn't you hear me?" Chris walked over to his friend and clapped a hand on his shoulder. "Dave, what's the—"

He stopped short. As he looked into Dave's locker, he saw an open shoebox. It was filled with pill vials, hypodermic needles, and tiny brown bottles.

Dave looked at his friend then down at the floor. "I have to drop out," he said, his voice shaking. "There's no way I can pass."

The History of Drug Testing

Steroids may produce visible effects on a user's body, including acne, hair loss, darkened skin, jaundice (yellowed skin caused by liver ailments), swollen legs and feet, and trembling. Women who use steroids may have facial hair growth and unusually deep voices. But to confirm steroid use, tests must be performed. Because many athletic officials and natural athletes believe that steroids give users an unfair advantage, steroid testing is performed at many athletic events.

Drug testing of Olympic athletes began in the 1968 Olympic Winter Games. But an accurate test for steroids was not developed until 1973. Specific testing for steroids began with the 1976 Olympics.

Drug testing has also come into professional sports.

In Great Britain, professional soccer players have been tested since 1979. The National Basketball Association in the United States introduced drug testing for its players in 1983. Professional baseball introduced testing in 1986. And at Wimbledon and the U.S. Open, tennis players were first tested for drug use in 1986. The penalties for steroid use vary from one organization to another, but most sports ban a user from competition for a specified length of time. Repeat offenders may face a lifetime ban from their sport.

How Effective Are Drug Tests?

There are several types of drug tests, including lie detector tests and tests that use blood, urine, and hair samples. Hair sample testing is still in developmental stages, and lie detector tests are considered unreliable. Blood tests may be the most precise, because they can pick up traces of drugs taken as long as two months earlier. Urine tests are the most widely used, however, because urine is easier to collect and to analyze than blood. At the Olympic Games, both urine and blood tests are used.

The International Olympic Committee conducts urine and blood tests using a chemical procedure called gas chromatography–mass spectrometry (GS/MS). First, a urine or blood sample is screened to determine if any banned substances are present. If the sample tests positive, the test goes on to identify the substance or substances.

In what was the biggest story of the 1988 Summer Olympics in Seoul, South Korea, Ben Johnson, a

Canadian track-and-field athlete, was caught with a positive drug test. After his world-record finish of 9.79 seconds in the 100-meter race, Johnson had to give up his gold medal. It went to his longtime rival, the American sprinter Carl Lewis, who had finished second.

Since drug testing began, athletes have done just about anything to get around the rules. In one case, a Canadian track coach ordered a female competitor to drink a pint of vinegar, thinking it would mask the presence of the anabolic steroids she had been taking. In another case, an East German steroid user was caught because the doctor who administered her drugs made a mistake. The doctor injected the drug into her body fat, which retains traces of drugs longer than muscle, instead of into her muscle.

These athletes were caught. But others are not. While certain injectable steroids can be picked up in a test months after the last injection, oral drugs can be out of the system a few days after they are taken. Some drugs can be taken up to several hours before the test is scheduled, which is usually the day of the competition. And other drugs can mask the presence of a steroid in the urine or blood.

The Future of Drug Testing

The best way to catch drug users is to do spot drug tests with frequent testing during the off-season as well as during competition.

In 1989 the U.S. Olympic Committee and the Soviet Union signed an agreement that allowed athletic officials from one country to demand drug testing of an athlete from the other country. Under this agreement, an athlete with a positive test may be banned from competition for two years. With a second offense, an athlete can be banned for life.

Drug testing is controversial for several reasons. Many athletes, especially natural athletes, feel that urine tests are an invasion of privacy. Some people feel that it is unfair to test only athletes, since nonathletes also abuse steroids. If everyone cannot be tested, these people argue, no one should be tested. In addition, testing is expensive. But steroid testing is likely to continue as long as organizations can afford to test. Most sports officials feel they simply must do something to ensure fairness in competition.

In the past several years, some schools have begun testing their athletes for drugs. The NCAA tests players after championship events. Even a few U.S. high schools have started drug testing programs. Although most school districts cannot afford to spend the money for testing, many are still considering testing for the future. High school students are at a great risk to develop health problems from steroid use. And, of course, if some school athletes use steroids while others do not, competition between schools is unfair.

5
Other Drugs in Sports

As Brian and Jason walked home from wrestling practice, they talked about next Saturday's meet against their crosstown rivals.

"I'm not eating anything but milk and steak for the next few days," said Brian. "I have to make weight." He looked longingly at the bakery as they walked past.

"Hey, would you wait up a minute?" Jason asked. "I need to find a bathroom." He ducked into the bakery before Brian could say anything.

A few minutes later, Jason came back out of the bakery.

"What's the matter with you?" Brian asked. "That's the third time you've had to go in the last hour."

Jason didn't answer right away. He looked from side to side. "Do you promise not to tell?"

34

Brian nodded his head, though he had no idea what Jason was about to tell him.

"Okay," said Jason, unzipping his gym bag. "Look."

Brian looked into the bag. Amid the jumble of wrestling shoes and clothes was a small blue box. The name *Diurex* was printed on it.

"What's that?" he asked, but then he remembered. He'd seen that same blue box in the drugstore; it contained diuretic pills. A television commercial rang in his head: "For the elimination of excess water weight."

"So that's why you've been going to the bathroom so much lately!" said Brian.

"Sssssh! I don't want anyone to find out," said Jason. "I've got to make my weight class. And my father will kill me if I lose the match this weekend. He's invited the whole family to watch. I've tried not to eat, but I lose all my strength. I have to take them!" he said, zipping his bag shut.

The History of Other Drugs in Sports

Steroid abuse is not the only drug problem affecting athletes. Drugs have been used to improve athletic performance for centuries. Some experts believe that frequent use of other drugs encouraged the atmosphere that has made steroid use so common. Drug use was reported in ancient Greece's original Olympic Games in 776 B.C. We also know that as far back as 600 B.C., Roman gladiators took drugs—probably **stimulants** (chemicals that excite the brain)—so they could continue to fight even after being injured.

In the 19th century, athletes experimented with many different kinds of drugs—caffeine, opium, nitroglycerine, and strychnine, to name a few. Marathon bicycle races were popular, and many cyclists consumed large quantities of nitroglycerine and ether so that they could stay awake through the six-day-long races. French cyclists and lacrosse players used cocaine during practice and matches. And strychnine was given as a stimulant to boxers, as well as regular massages with a cream of cocoa butter and cocaine, which served as an **anesthetic**, or painkiller, on the skin surface.

Drug use continued to increase unchecked until the 1960 Rome Olympics, when Knud Jensen, a Danish cyclist, collapsed and died during opening-day races. An autopsy found **amphetamines** in his system. The International Olympic Committee responded by requiring the first drug tests at the 1964 Olympics in Tokyo.

Common Drugs Used by Athletes

Since the 1960s, when widespread use of drugs was first being reported, drugs have become more sophisticated and more varied. Steroids are just the tip of the iceberg.

Beta-blockers are used by doctors to treat high blood pressure, heartbeat irregularities, and a common heart ailment called angina. Beta-blockers prolong the time between heartbeats. Athletes who need hand and arm steadiness—for sports such as archery and pool—have been known to take beta-blockers. Beta-blockers also lessen anxiety and help prevent stage fright, a common problem in sports competition. Beta-blockers have been banned by the IOC and the NCAA, and they can be detected by drug testing. They can be very dangerous to a person with an already slow heartbeat. The drugs can cause heart failure and bronchospasm—a sudden tightening of the airways to the lungs—as well as insomnia, depression, and impotence.

Diuretics promote urination and are used to treat certain heart and kidney ailments and high blood pressure. They are sometimes used by wrestlers, bodybuilders, weightlifters, gymnasts, and jockeys, who need to "make weight," that is, to lose a certain number of pounds in order to fit into a competition weight class. Frequent urination removes fluid from the body and causes weight loss. Some athletes have used diuretics to cover up their use of other banned drugs. The increased urine can dilute other drugs, making them more difficult to detect in tests. But diuretics themselves can be detected with drug testing, and they have been banned by the IOC and the NCAA. Using diuretics can even backfire, causing an athlete to become seriously dehydrated. Other side effects are skin rashes, stomach problems, muscle cramps, and blood disorders.

Caffeine is a stimulant used by athletes to increase alertness. Caffeine increases the metabolism of fat, providing a slow release of energy to the muscles. It is a legal drug that millions of people ingest daily in coffee, tea, soda pop, and chocolate. It also comes in pill form that can be purchased without a prescription.

But the IOC and the NCAA ban caffeine in high amounts. The drug can easily be detected in a drug test. Too much caffeine can cause nervousness, insomnia, and an inability to focus. In addition, caffeine has a diuretic effect that can dehydrate an athlete.

Human growth hormone (hGH), an injectable liquid, is a growth hormone produced naturally by the body's **pituitary gland**, a pea-sized gland located under the brain. The hormone used to be extracted from the pituitary gland of cadavers (dead bodies) to treat growth hormone deficiency. In this pure form, hGH was very expensive, and it was not commonly abused. But since pituitary-derived products were banned in the United States in 1985, synthetic forms of the hormone have become available. The use of synthetic hGH among athletes is on the rise. Although blood or urine tests cannot detect its use, hGH is banned by the U.S. Olympic Committee and the NCAA. Any evidence confirming hGH use will result in the same penalties as the use of any other banned drug. Users believe that hGH increases muscle strength, but there is no solid evidence that supports this. People who use hGH may develop a physical disorder called **acromegaly**, causing overgrowth of the bones. Facial features thicken, and the hands, feet, jaw, and brow grow disproportionately large. Acromegaly is irreversible in both men and women.

Though **blood doping** does not involve the use of drugs, some athletes think it provides an unfair advantage to athletes who practice it. Also called "boosting" or "blood packing," blood doping is the term for the infusion of extra red blood cells into an athlete's body. A pint or two of blood is removed from an athlete up to three months before an athletic event. The red blood cells are separated from the rest of the blood and frozen until needed again. Meanwhile, the athlete's body works hard to replace the blood cells that were removed. Then, a few days before the event, the stored red cells are thawed and injected into the athlete's body.

People who dope their blood believe that since red blood cells carry oxygen through the body, boosting endurance and stamina, more blood cells and more oxygen will enhance their performance. The technique is used by athletes in sports such as long-distance running, cross-country skiing, and cycling. Evidence seems to indicate that blood doping works. Several U.S. cyclists even admitted to blood doping after an impressive showing at the 1984 Olympic Games in Los Angeles. But blood doping presents dangers. Excess red cells thicken blood, so that it clots more easily and causes the body's blood pressure to rise. Blood doping can cause an athlete to push too hard and strain the heart. The blood transfusion procedure can also put a doper at risk for diseases, including AIDS. Hypodermic needles, used for the transfusion of the blood, can spread germs if they are not clean. And blood itself can carry diseases. Some dopers use donated blood cells instead of their own, putting themselves at an even greater risk of contracting a serious disease.

Blood doping is banned by the NCAA and the IOC. Although blood or urine tests cannot detect blood doping, any evidence confirming the procedure's use can cause an athlete to be penalized.

Brake drugs are sometimes used by young female gymnasts who want to retain their small stature. Brake drugs actually stop the growth that happens when a girl reaches puberty. Brake drugs are made from the female sex hormones called estrogens, and they are similar in structure to birth control pills. The extra estrogen works to suppress **ovulation,** or the release of an egg from the girl's ovary. Ovulation triggers changes in a girl's body—widening her hips and causing her breasts to develop and her bones to grow. As long as ovulation is suppressed, a girl isn't able to enter puberty. Her growth from a girl into a woman is "braked." This delay allows her to compete as a gymnast for a few years longer with a body that is familiar to her. Researchers don't yet know the extent of the damage that this delayed growth can cause to a woman's body later on.

6
Training without Drugs

Steve sat on a bench in the empty gym with his head in his hands. The cheers that had filled the room just 15 minutes earlier still rang in his ears—cheers for the other school's team.

How had it happened? Tonight's game was the last JV basketball game of the season, and Steve had blown his last chance to win a game for his team. He had control, but he wasn't fast enough, and he couldn't make a dunk shot like some of the other guys could. He was just too small.

Steve cupped his chin in his hands and stared at the orange balls piled up in the corner of the gym. He replayed the game over and over in his mind. When Coach Williams sat down on the bench next to him, Steve didn't look up.

"So you're thinking about next year, right?" the coach asked him.

Steve looked down at his shoes. "I don't know if I'll be back," he said. "I don't think I can make varsity. Unless—" He stopped.

"Unless what?"

"Oh, I don't know, it seems so unfair," Steve said. "All the other guys are so much better than me, and the guys on the other team—" Steve searched for the right words. "They have more help than any of us."

"You mean they take drugs? Steroids?"

Steve sighed. "Yeah."

"And you've been thinking about it?"

"Yeah."

Coach Williams put his hand on Steve's shoulder. "I'll tell you a secret, Steve. No one is supposed to know until September, but I'll let you in on it now. Our division is going to start drug testing next fall."

"Yeah? But guys will still cheat."

"Some will try. But it's going to be random testing, so we think a lot of the users will be scared into going clean. The school board and the athletic department have been talking about testing for a year now. We're going to completely overhaul training methods for every team in the school. If it works here, the plan will go into effect all over the state.

"Besides," the coach continued, "you've got to think about the future. Steroids might get you through high school. But you could develop health problems later and have them for the rest of your life. Is that worth a couple years of glory?"

"But I'm *not* going to play for just a couple years." Steve said. "I want to play pro ball!"

The coach smiled. "All the more reason to stay healthy," he said. "You have a better chance of getting to the pros without drugs."

Drug-Free Athletes

It *is* possible to train effectively for a sport without using drugs. In fact, more and more athletes are going drug-free. They are finding ways of becoming stronger without endangering their health. And they are happier and more confident knowing that they are competing honestly. To develop their natural abilities to the fullest, drug-free athletes need to be conscientious about diet, sleep, and training.

Diet

Eating foods that will maximize your potential takes long-range planning. Planning is best done with the advice of your doctor or your coach. He or she can help you plan a diet for every day, as well as for special pre-competition meals.

Protein and fat are vital to good health and strong athletic performance, but carbohydrates are an athlete's main fuel. They are carried by the blood to the body's cells. Excess carbohydrates are stored in the muscles for future use, when energy runs low.

There are two kinds of carbohydrates—simple and complex. *Simple carbohydrates* are found in foods such as cookies, white bread, and white rice. Simple carbohydrates enter the bloodstream immediately and provide the body with a sudden boost of energy. But the energy is depleted fast. *Complex carbohydrates* are found in foods such as oatmeal, brown rice, corn, potatoes, and other vegetables and fruit. Before they can enter the blood, complex carbohydrates must be broken into simple carbohydrates in the digestive system. Because this process is slow and gradual, complex carbohydrates supply a steady stream of energy to the muscles.

Ideally athletes should get 60–65 percent of their total calories from carbohydrates—preferably complex carbohydrates. They should get 15 percent of their calories from protein sources—such as cheese, eggs, meat, milk, grains, and nuts—and 20–25 percent from fat sources. Fat is contained in butter, meat, milk, eggs, and nuts.

It's also important to replace the fluids that are lost during hard athletic training. Athletes need to drink at least a quart of water each day in addition to other liquids. Studies show that most athletes only drink water to satisfy their thirst. This does not replace the amount of fluid their bodies lose during exercise. Dehydration, no matter how slight, can interfere with an athlete's training. If your energy level seems low and your diet follows the guidelines suggested here, try increasing the amount of water you drink every day.

Sleep

Sleep is a vital part of good athletic training. Sleep restores mental energy, repairs muscle cells damaged during training, and provides adequate energy for workouts the next day. Eight hours of sleep a night is usually sufficient for the teenage athlete, but some young people need more sleep when their workouts are particularly intense. A brief nap during the day will help to restore energy for regular workouts.

Training

Your coach knows a lot about the kind of training that will prepare you for your particular sport. He or she can make sure that you don't overtrain and become injured. A balance of aerobic exercise, strength training, exercise drills, and rest is the best formula for athletic success.

In addition, sports psychology studies have led to new, important training routines for the drug-free athlete. Many coaches are using positive imagery, goal setting, relaxation training, and assertiveness training as ways to improve athletes' performances.

Positive imagery combines deep breathing exercises and visualization of the athletic event before it occurs—step by step, stroke by stroke. Athletes imagine themselves crossing the finish line, making the winning basket, or setting a new record. In *goal setting*, an athlete identifies goals and the steps needed to achieve them, then tackles them step by step. *Relaxation training* helps keep muscles from becoming overtense and enhances concentration. *Assertiveness training* helps athletes to control anger, to think positively, and to cope with the fear of disapproval. Many athletes swear by these methods. They have discovered that the power of the mind is just as important as muscle strength when it comes to performing at their best.

Drugs are a constant temptation to athletes, especially when competitors are using them. But you *can* train and compete successfully without drugs. And despite the large number of athletes who use drugs, many others do not. More and more athletes, as they learn more about the dangers of drugs and the benefits of alternative training, are turning away from drugs. They are learning that you don't have to use steroids or other drugs to become a better athlete.

For Further Reading

Asken, Michael J. *Dying to Win: The Athlete's Guide to Safe and Unsafe Drugs in Sports*. Reston, VA: Acropolis Books, 1988.

Berger, Gilda. *Drug Abuse: The Impact on Society*. New York: Franklin Watts, 1988.

Dolan, Edward F., Jr. *Drugs in Sports*. New York: Franklin Watts, 1986.

Donohoe, Tom, and Johnson, Neil. *Foul Play: Drug Abuse in Sports*. Cambridge, MA: Basil Blackwell, 1988.

Francis, Charlie. *Speed Trap: A Track Coach's Explosive Account of How the World's Greatest Athletes Win*. New York: St. Martin's Press, 1991.

Harris, Jonathan. *Drugged Athletes: The Crisis in American Sports*. New York: Four Winds Press, 1987.

Monroe, Judy. *Drug Testing*. Riverside, NJ: Crestwood House, 1990.

Nuwer, Hank. *Steroids*. New York: Franklin Watts, 1990.

Talmadge, Katherine S. *Focus on Steroids*. Frederick, MD: Twenty-first Century Books, 1991.

Tricker, Ray. *Athletes at Risk: Drugs and Sport*. Dubuque, IA: Wm. C. Brown, 1990.

Resources

For more information about steroids, you can contact one of these organizations:

American College of Sports Medicine
401 W. Michigan
Indianapolis, IN 46202-3233
317-637-9200

Athletic Commission of New York State
270 Broadway
New York, NY 10007
212-417-5700

The Athletic Congress of the USA (Track-and-Field)
1 Hoosier Dome, Suite 140
Indianapolis, IN 46225
317-261-0500

Drug Abuse Information Treatment and Referral
    Hotline
1-800-662-4357

International Amateur Athletic Federation
3 Hans Crescent
Knightbridge
London SW1X OLN
England

National Association on Drug Abuse Problems
335 Lexington Ave.
New York, NY 10017
212-986-1170

National Clearinghouse for Drug Abuse Information
P.O. Box 2345
Rockville, MD 20852
301-443-6500

National Institute on Drug Abuse
5600 Fishers Lane
Rockville, MD 20857
301-443-2403

Teen-age Assembly of America
441 Mananai Place, No. E
Honolulu, HI 96818
808-486-5959

United States Athletic Association
3735 Lakeland Ave. N., Suite 230
Minneapolis, MN 55422
612-522-5844

United States Olympic Committee
1750 East Boulder Street
Colorado Springs, CO 80909
719-632-5551

Glossary

acromegaly: a physical disorder characterized by overgrowth of the bones in the hands, feet, and face

adrenal glands: small, hormone-producing organs located near the kidneys

amphetamines: drugs that increase physical and mental activity by stimulating the brain

anabolic steroids: synthetic steroids that promote muscle growth

anesthetic: a substance that relieves pain

beta-blockers: drugs that reduce the heartbeat rate and lower blood pressure

blood doping: the infusion of extra red blood cells into the body

brake drugs: drugs made from estrogens that suppress ovulation and stop the normal development of a girl's body at puberty

caffeine: a stimulant that is found in many kinds of coffee, tea, and carbonated drinks, and is also manufactured in pill form

carbohydrates: a class of food essential to the body that includes sugars and starches. Carbohydrates are the main source of energy for animals and plants.

cartilage: a rubbery tissue found at the end of bones

corticosteroids: natural steroids, released by the body's adrenal glands, that help to regulate protein and carbohydrate metabolism

diuretics: drugs or other substances that increase the secretion of urine by the kidneys

estrogens: hormones that cause the growth and development of female secondary sexual characteristics

gynecomastia: breast development in boys and men

hepatitis: inflammation of the liver

hormones: chemical substances, produced naturally within the body or synthetically, that regulate functions such as growth, sexual development, and reproduction

human growth hormone (hGH): a growth hormone produced naturally by the body's pituitary gland, or a synthetic copy

hypodermic needle: a needle used to inject liquid beneath the skin

hypothalamus: an area of the brain that controls the secretion of steroids

impotence: the inability to achieve an erection

insomnia: the inability to sleep naturally

metabolism: the process by which the body turns food into energy and living tissue

ovaries: the female reproductive organs. Ovaries store and release eggs. They also secrete estrogens and progesterone.

ovulation: the release of an egg from the ovaries

pituitary gland: a pea-sized gland located under the brain, near the center of the skull, that secretes a number of hormones

placebo effect: physical improvement that is a result of confidence in a drug rather than any actual physical change

polypharmacy: the practice of taking many different drugs at the same time

primary sexual characteristics: the body's reproductive organs

progesterone: a hormone that prepares the uterus for pregnancy

secondary sexual characteristics: the gender-related physical characteristics that appear at puberty, such as breasts in females and facial hair in males

sex steroids: steroids that influence the reproductive processes and control the development of secondary sexual characteristics. Progesterone and estrogens are female sex steroids. Testosterone is a male sex steroid.

stacking: the practice of taking several different steroids at the same time

sterility: the inability to reproduce

steroids: chemical compounds, either natural or synthetic, that influence the body's growth, metabolism, and blood chemistry. Hormones are one type of steroid.

stimulant: a chemical that increases physical and mental activity by exciting the brain

synthetic: made from chemicals in a laboratory; artificial

tendons: the tissues that attach muscles to bones

testes: the male reproductive glands that produce sperm. The testes also produce testosterone.

testosterone: a hormone that causes the growth and development of male secondary sexual characteristics

Index

acromegaly, 38
adrenal glands, 10
aggression, 12, 15, 23-24
anabolic steroids, 11-12, 15-19, 26; black market, 15, 18, 23, 27; defined, 11-12; laws against use, 26, 27, 28; medical uses of, 11, 15; side effects of, 18, 22-25, 30; testing for, 28, 30-33

beta-blockers, 36-37
blood doping, 38-39
bodybuilding, 15, 16, 27, 37
brake drugs, 40

caffeine, 36, 37-38
Canada, 27, 28, 32
carbohydrates, 10, 43-44
corticosteroids, 10, 11

dehydration, 37, 38, 44
diet, 43-44
diuretics, 37
drug testing, controversy over, 33; history of, 30-31; in Olympic Games, 28, 30, 31-32, 33, 36, 37, 38, 39-40; in NCAA, 37, 38, 39-40; types of tests, 31

estrogens, 10, 40

Europe, 15

fat, 22, 32, 37; in diet, 43, 44
football, 15, 16, 28

gymnastics, 37, 40
gynecomastia, 22

hormones, 10, 38, 40
human growth hormone (hGH), 38
hypothalamus, 10

International Amateur Athletic Federation (IAAF), 28
International Olympic Committee (IOC), 28, 31, 36, 37, 38, 39-40

Jensen, Knud, 36
Johnson, Ben, 31-32

metabolism, 10, 37
Mexico, 27

National Basketball Association (NBA), 31
National Collegiate Athletic Association (NCAA), 28, 37, 38, 39-40
National Football League (NFL), 16, 28

Learn to cope with other modern problems in:

Celebrate You!
Building Your Self-Esteem
by Julie Tallard Johnson

Eating Disorders
A Question and Answer Book about Anorexia Nervosa and
Bulimia Nervosa
by Ellen Erlanger

Family Violence
How to Recognize and Survive It
by Janice E. Rench

Making Friends, Finding Love
A Book about Teen Relationships
by Julie Tallard Johnson

Teen Pregnancy
by Sonia Bowe-Gutman

Teen Sexuality
Decisions and Choices
by Janice E. Rench

Teen Suicide
A Book for Friends, Family, and Classmates
by Janet Kolehmainen and Sandra Handwerk

Understanding Mental Illness
For Teens Who Care about Someone with Mental Illness
by Julie Tallard Johnson